Penguin Readers

D1254038

LIFE IN
SPACE

LEVEL

2

WRITTEN BY CATRIN MORRIS
SERIES EDITOR: SORREL PITTS

PENGUIN BOOKS

UK | USA | Canada | Ireland | Australia
India | New Zealand | South Africa

Penguin Books is part of the Penguin Random House group of companies
whose addresses can be found at global.penguinrandomhouse.com.
www.penguin.co.uk www.puffin.co.uk www.ladybird.co.uk

First published 2020
001

Text written by Catrin Morris
Text copyright © Penguin Books Ltd, 2020

Printed in China

A CIP catalogue record for this book is available from the British Library

ISBN: 978-0-241-37523-5

All correspondence to:
Penguin Books
Penguin Random House Children's
One Embassy Gardens, New Union Square
5 Nine Elms Lane, London SW8 5DA

Contents

New words

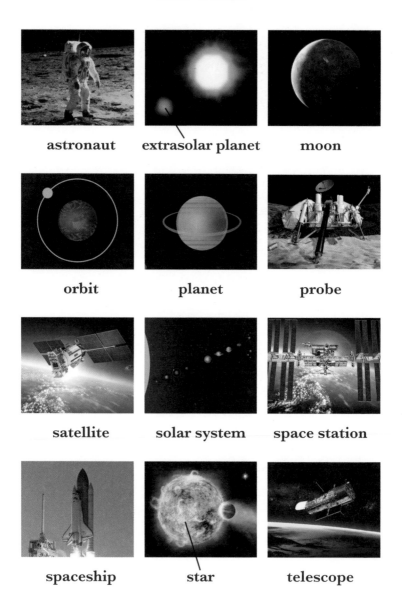

astronaut   extrasolar planet   moon

orbit   planet   probe

satellite   solar system   space station

spaceship   star   telescope

Note about the book

Before people went into space in **spaceships***, they sent machines into space. After that, they sent animals into space in the machines.

First, only Russian and American **astronauts** travelled into space. Now astronauts from lots of different countries go to space. They teach us more about **life** on Earth and in space.

Before-reading questions

1 Look at the cover of the book. What do you know about space?
2 How many planets are in Earth's solar system?
3 Are there other planets in space? What do we call these planets?
4 What is an "astronaut"?
5 How do astronauts go into space?
6 Which countries went into space in the past?
7 Which countries go into space now?
8 What is an "alien"?
9 Is there life in space, do you think?

*Definitions of words in **bold** can be found in the glossary on pages 62–64.

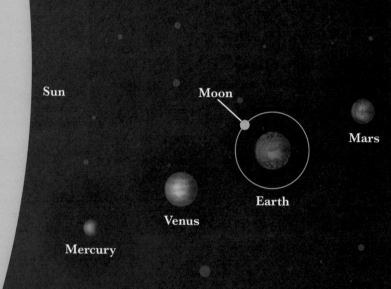

Sun

Moon

Mars

Earth

Venus

Mercury

The Earth's solar system

CHAPTER ONE

Machines in space

The Earth's **solar system** has eight **planets**. These planets **orbit** the Sun. Some of these planets have **moons**, but some do not.

There are also lots of **extrasolar planets** in space. These planets orbit different suns. Extrasolar planets are very **far** from the Earth. People cannot visit them, but maybe one day machines will visit them.

Sending machines into space is easier than sending people there. In 1957, Russia sent the first **satellite** into space. It was called Sputnik 1.

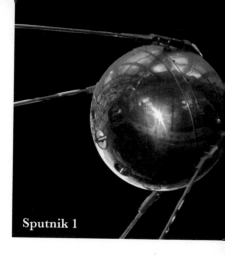
Sputnik 1

A satellite is a **spaceship**. Sometimes there are no people on it. It orbits a planet, a **star** or a moon. Today, lots of countries send satellites into space. Satellites are **light**, and they can fly very high.

A satellite in space

They often carry cameras and **telescopes**. They can send important photos and messages back to Earth.

Probes are special spaceships. They can travel millions of miles into space. But they can also **land** in difficult places and do **experiments**. Then the probes send messages about these places back to Earth.

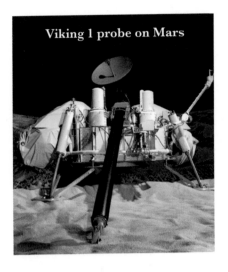

Viking 1 probe on Mars

NASA is the National Aeronautics and Space Administration in the United States of America. Viking 1 and 2 were NASA's first probes to land on a planet. They landed on Mars in 1976.

Viking 1 and 2 took photos, did experiments and looked for **life** on Mars.

NASA's Voyager 1 and 2 probes left Earth in 1977. They studied Jupiter, Saturn, Uranus and Neptune.

Now these two probes are learning more about space.

In 1997, the Cassini-Huygens space probe travelled to Saturn.

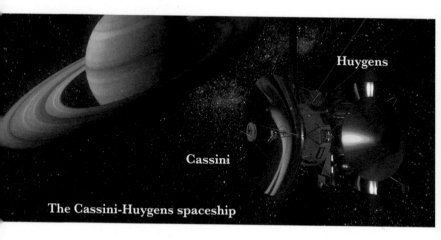

The Cassini-Huygens spaceship

The Cassini part of the spaceship was a probe. It went around Saturn, and it found new moons and seas. The Huygens part of the spaceship was also a probe. It landed on Titan, Saturn's largest moon.

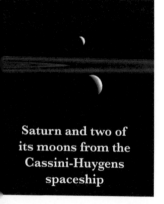

Saturn and two of its moons from the Cassini-Huygens spaceship

Cassini-Huygens was very big and heavy, and it travelled 7,800,000,000 **kilometres**. It stayed in space for twenty years and took 453,048 photos. It cost $3,900,000,000, and more than 5,000 people worked on it.

The Spirit and Opportunity probes

In 2003, NASA sent two more probes to Mars. Spirit and Opportunity landed on Mars in 2004.

They could move over the planet better than other probes before them, and they showed us something very important about Mars. There was water on Mars in the past. Did this mean there was life on Mars in the past, too?

NASA's other probe, Curiosity, is on Mars now.

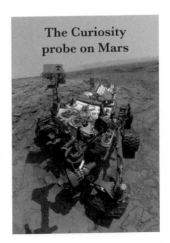

The Curiosity probe on Mars

It is exploring the ground, the **air** and the **rocks** on Mars. It is finding more **signs** that Mars was more friendly to life in the past.

Before machines went into space, people studied the solar system from the Earth with telescopes. But now telescopes also go into space.

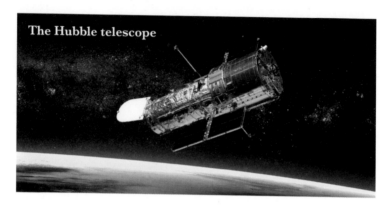

The Hubble telescope

Hubble was the first important telescope to be sent into space. NASA and the ESA (European Space Agency) sent Hubble into space in 1990.

Hubble goes around the Earth. We can see space better with Hubble. We saw extrasolar planets through Hubble. Hubble also studies stars before they die. When a star dies, there is sometimes a supernova.

Supernovae taught us something new about space. Space is growing very fast.

A supernova

There are a lot of other telescopes in space now. Chandra went into space in 1999. This telescope is learning new things about supernovae. Why do these stars die? Maybe Chandra can tell us.

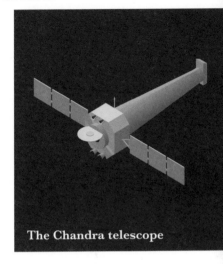
The Chandra telescope

Chandra can also find very dark places in space. These are called **black holes**. **Gravity** is very strong in black holes, and nothing can leave them. **Light** cannot leave them. Why is this? Maybe Chandra can help us understand black holes.

A black hole

The COROT telescope went into space in 2006. It is looking for extrasolar planets. Extrasolar planets are very far from the Earth. They are "light years" from the Earth. (One light year is 9,500,000,000,000 kilometres.)

A light year is how far light travels in a year. The nearest extrasolar planet is 4.2 light years away from the Earth.

The Kepler telescope went into space in 2009. The Earth is a small planet with a special **atmosphere**. Kepler is looking for other small planets with the same atmosphere as Earth. There is life on Earth. Maybe Kepler will find life on other planets, too.

Space through the Kepler telescope

CHAPTER TWO

People in space

Four years after the first
spaceship, Russia sent the
first **astronaut** into space.
In 1961, Yuri Gagarin
went into space on his
spaceship, Vostok 1.

Yuri Gagarin

Vostok 1 went around the
Earth for 108 minutes. A computer flew it from
Earth. This was because astronauts on Earth
were not happy about Gagarin's body in space
with no gravity. Vostok 1 flew very fast – at
27,400 kilometres per hour – and it flew 327
kilometres high in the sky.

Yuri Gagarin did not land back on Earth inside
Vostok 1. He came out of the spaceship with a
parachute before landing.

Yuri Gagarin's parachute

In 1969, America sent a spaceship to the Moon. The Moon is 384,400 kilometres away from the Earth and the spaceship took three days to get there. On 20th July, two astronauts landed on the Moon.

Neil Armstrong and Buzz Aldrin walked on the Moon, and they talked to people back on Earth. People from across the world watched and listened on their televisions.

Buzz Aldrin on the Moon

NASA and the ESA would like to send astronauts to some of the other planets in our solar system. But this is not easy, because the spaceship has to travel for many months.

Mars

78,340,000 kilometres from Earth

Earth

Taking off and landing can be difficult. Sometimes astronauts are not well, and sometimes they can have accidents.

A spaceship taking off from Earth

Space stations are helping us learn more about living in space. A space station is a big satellite. Astronauts can live on it for weeks or months. Russia built the first space station in 1971. It was called Salyut 1.

Salyut 1 stayed in space for 175 days. Three Russian astronauts flew to it on a spaceship and lived there for three weeks. They later died in an accident on their spaceship.

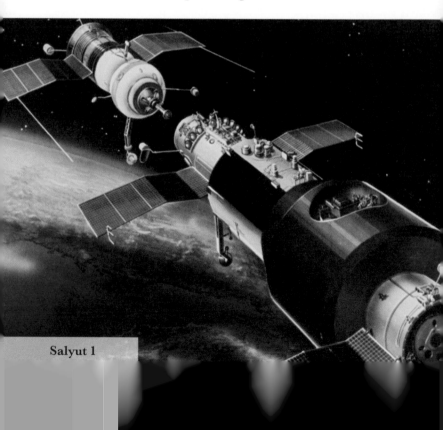

Salyut 1

Skylab 1 was America's first space station. It took off into space in 1973.

Skylab 1 was very important. It stayed in space for 171 days. Three groups of astronauts stayed on the space station for 28, 59 and 84 days. The astronauts learned a lot about living together in space. They had special beds and toilets, and a special kitchen.

The astronauts came back to Earth. Then the space station came back into the Earth's atmosphere in 1979. Most of Skylab 1 went into the sea, but some small bits landed in Australia. People found these bits of the space station and kept them.

Skylab 1

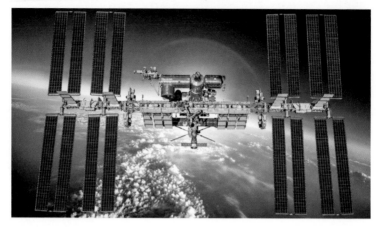

The ISS

The ISS (the International Space Station) went into space in 2000. It goes around the Earth, and sometimes you can see it in the sky.

It can look very bright, and it moves very fast. A plane flies at 926 kilometres per hour. The space station flies at 28,000 kilometres per hour. Six astronauts from different countries live on the ISS together.

Life is not easy on the space station. There is no gravity, and your body is in the air.

Astronauts in the International Space Station

20

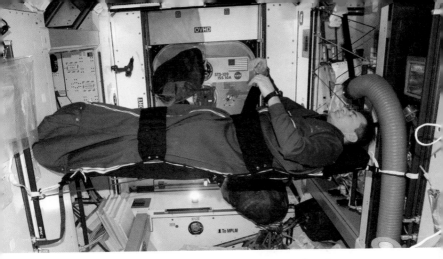

Sleeping in the International Space Station

Eating, sleeping and moving are as important for people in space as on Earth. But doing these things can be difficult in space.

The Sun comes up every ninety minutes in space. Astronauts cannot sleep, because it is too light. They have to put something over their eyes to stop the light.

Eating can also be difficult. You sometimes have to add water to food before you can eat it. Sometimes you are not very hungry, because the food is not very good. No gravity can be bad for people, too. After only a few days in space, your body is not as strong as it is on Earth. You have to move a lot so your body can stay strong.

CHAPTER THREE

Is there life in space?

In the past, some people saw **UFOs** (Unidentified Flying Objects) in the sky.

Were these UFOs spaceships from other planets? Were there **aliens** on these spaceships?

You can read stories and see photos of these UFOs in the news. But are the stories true? What did the people really see? Is there life on other planets? We do not know.

Water on Earth

Maybe we first have to ask, "Why is there life on Earth?"

There are seas and rivers everywhere on Earth. Maybe life on Earth began in the sea, because living things need water. Now **astronomers** are looking for other planets with lots of water.

The Earth's atmosphere has the right air, and living things need this air. The Earth also has lots of rocks.

Astronomers are looking for other planets with lots of rocks. Maybe there are signs of life in the rocks. They are looking for planets with the right atmosphere, too.

Venus

Astronomers are also looking for planets with the same weather as Earth.

Things cannot live on Venus, because it is too hot. It is too near the Sun. Maybe things cannot live on Mars, because it is too cold. It is far from the Sun.

The Earth has spring, summer, autumn and winter. The atmosphere on Earth changes in summer and winter. More things grow in hot summers than in cold winters.

Astronomers are studying the atmosphere on some extrasolar planets with a special new telescope. They want to find planets with the same atmosphere as the Earth. Maybe things can live and grow there, too.

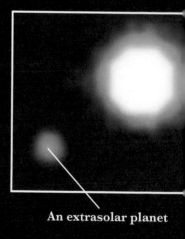

An extrasolar planet

Astronomers are also listening for radio **signals** from other planets. In the 1960s, an American astronomer called Frances Drake started listening for them with a radio telescope. He heard some radio signals, but they came from planes in the sky.

Radio signals

A radio telescope

In the 1970s, NASA started listening for radio signals, too. But they did not hear any radio signals from aliens. In the 1990s, NASA stopped listening to the signals. But, now, many other astronomers are listening for radio signals, and better computers can help the astronomers.

Astronomers found lots of possible new extrasolar planets in other solar systems.

Light signals

They are using the Kepler telescope for this.

Kepler looks at groups of stars in space. It watches them for lots of years.

Sometimes a "thing" moves across a star. And then that star is not as bright.

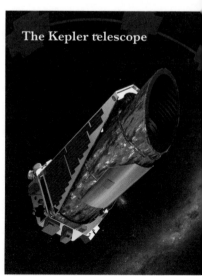

The Kepler telescope

But are these "things" planets? Astronomers do not always know.

CHAPTER FOUR

Where are we looking for life?

Astronomers often look for life on Mars. They first saw Mars through a telescope from Earth. Mars looks red because of its rocks.

The atmosphere on Mars hits the rocks, and the rocks go red. This is called oxidation.

In the past, Mars was warmer, and there was water on the ground. But where did the water go? Some of it is now **ice** on the high ground. Some of it went into the atmosphere. Some of it stayed under the rocks on Mars.

In July 2018, the ESA Mars Express orbiter found lots of water under the ground on Mars.

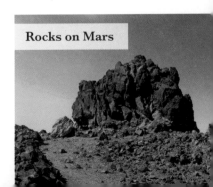

Rocks on Mars

27

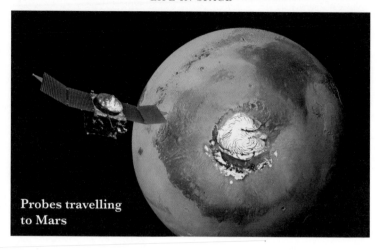

Probes travelling to Mars

Maybe there are small living things in Mars's rocks today. Maybe there are living things in the water under the ground on Mars. NASA and the ESA are going to send new probes to Mars. They will find rocks and bring them back to Earth.

The probes will take rocks from Mars.

Maybe later more planets will get warm because the Sun is getting bigger and hotter.

Maybe Mars will get hotter and have water on its ground again. Maybe there will be rivers and seas on Mars – and new life, too.

Astronomers are also looking for life on moons. Jupiter is the biggest planet in the solar system. Seventy-nine moons orbit Jupiter; the biggest ones are the Galilean moons: Io, Europa, Ganymede and Callisto.

Jupiter and its moons

The Galilean moons

Io   Europa   Ganymede   Callisto

The Italian astronomer Galileo Galilei first saw these four moons in 1610. You can see them with a telescope.

Jupiter's moons look cold and dead, but they are not. Io is very hot and dry. It has **volcanoes**. And things can live and grow near volcanoes. But astronomers are looking for life on Jupiter, not its moons.

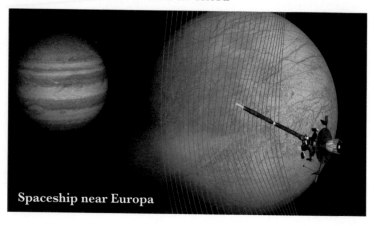

Spaceship near Europa

Most of Europa has ice on it. But maybe there is warm water under the ice.

Ganymede is the biggest moon in the solar system. It is bigger than the planet Mercury. Ganymede has a lot of ice and rocks on it. This is the same as the Earth. Maybe Ganymede had life on it in the past.

Callisto is Jupiter's second-largest moon and the third-largest moon in our solar system. It has lots of rocks and ice but no volcanoes on it. Maybe there is sea under the rocks, and life in that sea.

30

Astronomers would like to look for life on Europa more than the other Galilean moons. This is because Europa is much smaller than Earth but possibly has more water on it. NASA's Galileo spaceship saw a lot of water in Europa's ice. Now astronomers want to look at it more closely.

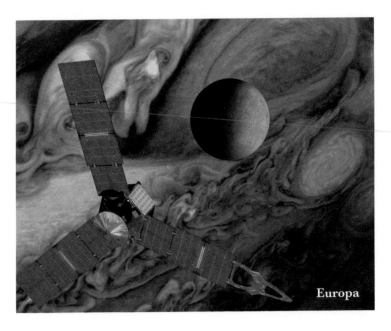

Europa

Exploring water under ice is very difficult in space. NASA's new Europa Clipper satellite is going to orbit Jupiter. It wants to take some water from Europa. Astronomers will do experiments with this water and look for life in it.

Saturn

Saturn is the next biggest planet in the solar system after Jupiter, but things cannot live on Saturn. It has a lot of hot air, and ice and rocks orbit it.

But a lot of moons orbit it, too. Maybe things can live on Saturn's moons.

Titan is Saturn's biggest moon. Titan's atmosphere has a lot of **gas** in it. Earth has a lot of gas, too. There is sometimes heavy rain, but the rain on Titan is not water rain.

There are rivers and seas of gas on Titan, but there is not any water. It is too cold for water. Maybe things can live and grow on Titan anyway.

Titan

32

Enceladus is Saturn's brightest moon. A lot of Enceladus is ice and gas. But there is also water under the ice.

Water often comes through the ice on Enceladus. The Cassini spacecraft got some of this water, and astronomers did experiments with it. They found most of the things you need for life. Maybe there is life on Saturn's ice moon.

Enceladus

Astronomers are also looking for life on extrasolar planets. They would like to find an "Earth" in a different solar system. Maybe things are living and growing on it.

Finding extrasolar planets is not easy, because they are very far from Earth. But astronomers used space telescopes, and they saw a lot of extrasolar planets.

Some of these extrasolar planets are "hot Jupiters". They are too near their sun, and things cannot live or grow on them. But astronomers found other extrasolar planets, too.

In 2009, the COROT telescope found the extrasolar planet COROT-7b.

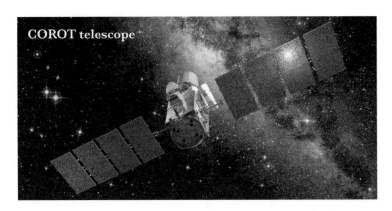

The planet had rocks on it. It is very small. It is about 500 light years away from the Earth. It orbits the star COROT-7 in about a day – the same time the Earth takes to orbit the Sun.

COROT-7b's sun is colder than our sun, but COROT-7b is very hot (2000 °C). It is too hot for life on COROT-7b, but maybe there are colder extrasolar planets out there.

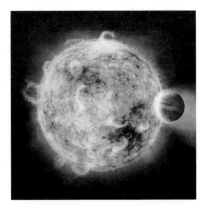

Extrasolar planet COROT-7b orbiting its sun

A planet must not be too near or too far from its sun for life.

In 2014, the Kepler telescope found an extrasolar planet called Kepler-186f. It is as small as the Earth, and it orbits a sun. It is not too near or too far from the sun. Maybe there is water and life on Kepler-186f.

Its sun is smaller and colder than the Earth's sun. This is good because small suns live longer than big suns. Maybe things can grow on their orbiting planets.

But we do not know, because we cannot visit Kepler-186f. It is 795 light years away from Earth.

Kepler-186f

Proxima b is the nearest extrasolar planet to Earth. Astronomers found it in 2016.

It also has rocks, and it is as big as the Earth. It goes around its sun, Proxima Centauri, every eleven days. It is nearer to Proxima Centauri than the Earth is to the Sun. But Proxima Centauri is not as hot as the Sun.

Is there water on the ground? Is there life on Proxima b? Astronomers do not know.

Proxima b is only four light years away. Maybe we can visit it one day.

CHAPTER FIVE

Life on Earth

Some astronomers are studying difficult places to live on Earth. Understanding life on Earth may help them find life in space.

Very small things live everywhere on Earth. They live in hot, dry places, and they live in cold, wet places. They live in very cold water and in very hot water.

They live in sea water and far under the sea, too.

Can small things live in difficult places on other planets, too?

Astronomers on Earth are studying different parts of space. This will help us travel in space.

The light from the Sun can be very strong on Earth, but it can be stronger on other planets. What does strong sun do to living things?

The atmosphere on some planets has lots of gas. Is this gas always bad for living things?

Gas is making the air dirty on Earth.

Gravity is very strong on Earth, but there is not as much gravity in space.

A group of astronomers is looking at stars in other solar systems. These solar systems are very far away from the Earth.

Astronomers are looking at stars in other solar systems.

NASA wants people to help them. They want them to look for new planets. You can watch videos from NASA's telescopes at *www.BackyardWorlds.org*. Then you can message NASA about them.

NASA is sending a new satellite into space called ICESat-2. It will look at the ice, water and rocks on Earth. Is the Earth colder or hotter now than in the past?

The satellite will also take a lot of photos of Earth, and it will look at its trees. This is because we see light differently through trees.

Scientists hope to find trees on other planets in other solar systems.

Earth's trees from a satellite

CHAPTER SIX

Tomorrow's space

NASA building in the USA

NASA and the ESA have lots of new machines in space now.

These machines can take astronauts to the ISS. One day they will be able to take astronauts to the Moon again.

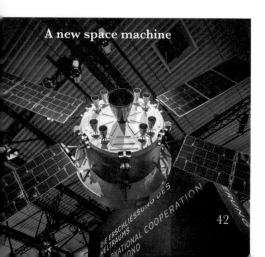

A new space machine

They can explore other planets, too, but they cannot take astronauts far into space. We must build better machines for this.

42

In 2018, NASA's Transiting Exoplanet Survey Satellite (TESS) went into space. The satellite is orbiting the Earth, and it is looking at 500,000 stars. It is looking for new extrasolar planets in different solar systems.

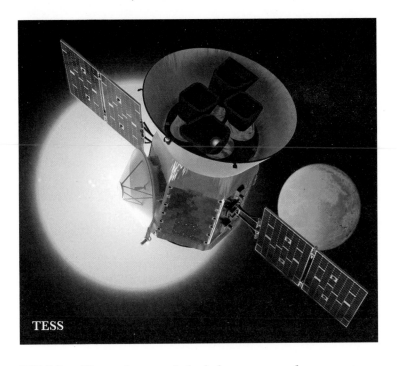

TESS

TESS will study much brighter stars than Kepler. It will also look at a part of the sky 400 times bigger. TESS will not only look for extrasolar planets. It will help astronomers learn about many new things in space.

NASA and the ESA are going to send the James Webb Space Telescope (JWST or Webb) into space in 2020.

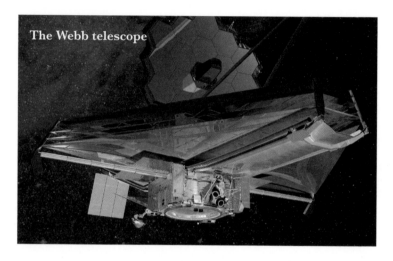

The Webb telescope

Webb will fly far away from the Earth. It will be the biggest telescope in space, and it will be able to answer many of our questions. It will learn more about how space started, and where stars and planets come from. It will tell us how fast space is growing.

Webb will also look at Kepler's work. It will study the ground, atmosphere, weather and moons of Kepler's possible new planets. And it will look for signs of life on them.

NASA is also sending two new machines to Mars. InSight is a probe that is now on Mars. It took off from Earth in May 2018.

InSight probe

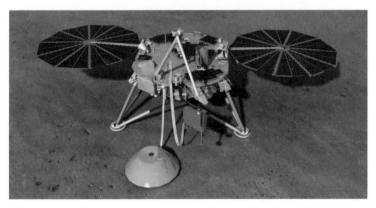

InSight probe

InSight will study Mars under the ground. It will tell us more about Mars in the past and now.

Mars 2020 probe

The probe Mars 2020 will take off from Earth in 2020. It will land on Mars and study the rocks and the ground.

Rocks on the ground on Mars

Later, another spaceship will carry the rocks back to Earth. Then astronomers can do more experiments on them. Maybe these experiments can answer more questions about Mars. Was there life on Mars in the past? Can there be life on Mars now?

Maybe these experiments can help astronauts to visit Mars one day.

The ESA is also sending a probe to Jupiter
and its moons in 2022. It will take 7.6 years
for the JUpiter ICy Moons Explorer (JUICE)
to travel to Jupiter.

The JUICE probe

It will orbit Jupiter for 3.5 years, and it will study
three of its ice moons: Ganymede, Callisto and
Europa. It will study the ice, the atmosphere and
the sea, and it will look for signs of life on them.

NASA's Orion spaceship travelling to the Moon

NASA is going to send astronauts back to the Moon on a spaceship. Then the astronauts can travel to other planets after the Moon.

It takes two or three days to get to the Moon from Earth. That is longer than to the ISS because the Moon is not as near to Earth.

Not only astronauts want to travel into space. Would you like to go to space in a spaceship? Soon you will be able to.

Blue Origin is going to fly people into space. They will fly 100 kilometres high for about ten minutes.

Blue Origin's New Glenn

SpaceX is going to fly people around the Moon. It will take two or three days to fly to the Moon and two or three days to fly back again.

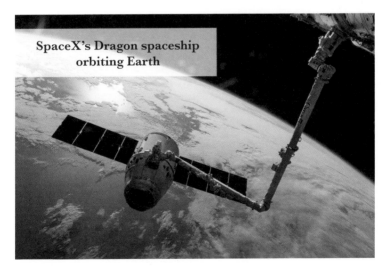

SpaceX's Dragon spaceship orbiting Earth

A Virgin Galactic spaceship

Virgin Galactic is planning to take six people into space, too.

They will fly for 2.5 hours and be in space with no gravity for six minutes. It will cost around $250,000 for each person.

NASA will open the ISS to tourists in 2020. Tourists will pay $35,000 for one night on the ISS.

CHAPTER SEVEN

Visiting other planets

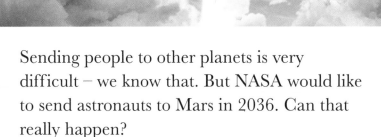

Sending people to other planets is very difficult – we know that. But NASA would like to send astronauts to Mars in 2036. Can that really happen?

First, they must build the right spaceship. It cannot be too heavy, or it will not take off from Earth. It must also be big and strong because it has to carry the astronauts and everything they will need. Then NASA must find the right astronauts.

The astronauts will be away from home for many years, and each one will have to do many jobs on the spaceship.

Mars is about 78,340,000 kilometres from the Earth.

Astronauts have to travel for about 260 days there and 260 days back. They would not be able to get any help from Earth because it is too far away.

They would be able to send a message to Earth from Mars, but Earth would only get the message after twenty minutes. They will have to wait another twenty minutes for an answer.

An astronaut coming back from space

Flying near the Sun can be bad for the body. What will years of light from the Sun and no gravity do to astronauts' bodies? And how will they feel after many months, or years, in space?

Astronauts have to stay in small places for many months or years. They cannot go out, and often they cannot sleep very well. Will they feel sad or tired? Will they get angry?

What happens after the spaceship lands on Mars? How long can the astronauts stay there? And how will they live on Mars?

Will they be able to grow food on Mars? Astronomers on Earth are planning for all these things. They are planning for the weather, too. It is very cold at night on Mars – about -100 °C.

People cannot live in this weather, because it is too cold for them. Scientists are trying to make special clothes for very cold weather.

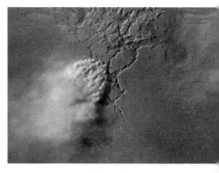

Mars weather system from space

Getting astronauts to Mars or to other planets will cost a lot of money. Who is going to pay for it? Do we have to visit Mars, and can we really use this money for travelling in space?

There are a lot of problems on Earth. People need schools, hospitals and houses, and these cost a lot of money, too.

But maybe we can learn a lot about the Earth from space. Maybe we can learn some new and important lessons.

And maybe this will help us to live better lives on Earth.

During-reading questions

Write the answers to these questions in your notebook.

CHAPTER ONE

1 What do the planets orbit?
2 What do extrasolar planets orbit?
3 Is it easier to send machines or people into space?
4 What is NASA?

CHAPTER TWO

1 Why was Yuri Gagarin special?
2 When did Neil Armstrong and Buzz Aldrin walk on the Moon?
3 How long did the journey take?
4 Why is the take-off difficult for astronauts?

CHAPTER THREE

1 What is a UFO?
2 Why is there life on Earth?
3 What are astronomers studying on extrasolar planets?
4 What does the Kepler telescope do?

CHAPTER FOUR

1 Which planet is red?
2 Which is the biggest planet in the solar system?
3 Which Galilean moon is very hot?
4 What is special about Proxima b?

CHAPTER FIVE

1 List the things astronomers are studying on or from the Earth.

CHAPTER SIX

1 How is TESS different from Kepler?
2 How long will Blue Origin fly people into space for?

CHAPTER SEVEN

1 What do NASA want to do in 2036?
2 What kind of spaceship will they need?

After-reading questions

1 What new things did you learn about our solar system?

2 What is the same or different about a satellite and a probe?

3 When does a supernova happen?

4 What are black holes, and what is special about them?

5 Name three important space telescopes and what they did or are doing.

6 What is difficult about life in space?

7 After reading this book, do you think there is life in space? Why/Why not?

8 Would you like to travel in space? Why/Why not?

Exercises

1 **Match the words with their definitions in your notebook.**
Example: 1–d

1	solar system	**a**	You can see things in space with this.
2	planet	**b**	a bright light in space
3	orbit	**c**	This machine goes into space.
4	moon	**d**	the Sun and all its planets
5	extrasolar planets	**e**	It orbits another sun.
6	spaceship	**f**	Mars is this.
7	star	**g**	how Earth moves around the Sun
8	telescope	**h**	It orbits a planet.

CHAPTERS ONE AND TWO

2 **Choose the correct word or phrase to complete the sentences in your notebook.**

1 Extrasolar planets are very *far* / **near** from the Earth.

2 In 1957, Russia sent the first **probe** / **satellite** into space. It was called Sputnik 1.

3 Cassini-Huygens was very big and heavy, and it travelled 7,800,000,000 **days** / **kilometres**.

4 The Curiosity probe is exploring the ground, the **air** / **signs** and the rocks on Mars.

5 Hubble also studies stars before they die. When a star dies, there is sometimes a **black hole** / **supernova**.

6 **Atmosphere** / **Gravity** is very strong in black holes, and nothing can leave them.

7 On 20th July, two astronauts **landed** / **took off** on the Moon.

58

3 Complete these sentences in your notebook, using the words from the box.

dry	cold	far	hot	near	atmosphere

1 There are seas and rivers everywhere on Earth, but other planets are too ...*dry*....

2 The Earth's .... has the right air for living things.

3 Things cannot live on Venus, because it is too ....

4 This is because Venus is too .... the Sun.

5 Maybe things cannot live on Mars, because it is too ....

6 Mars is .... from the Sun.

4 Complete the sentences in your notebook with the correct form of the verb.

Astronomers [1] ..*are looking*.. (look) for life on extrasolar planets. They [2] .... (want) to find an "Earth" in a different solar system. Maybe things are living and growing on it.

Finding extrasolar planets [3] .... (not be) easy, because they [4] .... (be) very far from Earth. But astronomers [5] .... (use) space telescopes, and they [6] .... (see) a lot of extrasolar planets.

Things cannot live or grow on "hot Jupiter" extrasolar planets. But astronomers [7] .... (find) other extrasolar planets, too.

5 **Write questions for these answers in your notebook.**

1 *When did TESS go into space?*

TESS went into space in 2018.

2 TESS is orbiting the Earth, and it is looking at 500,000 stars.

3 TESS is looking for new extrasolar planets in different solar systems.

4 The James Webb Space Telescope (Webb) is going into space in 2020.

5 NASA and the ESA are going to send Webb into space.

6 Webb will study the ground, atmosphere, weather and moons of Kepler's possible new planets.

6 **Write the correct verb form (present continuous or *will*) in your notebook.**

1 NASA *is sending* / **will send** two new machines to Mars.

2 InSight **is studying** / **will study** Mars under the ground, and it **is telling** / **will tell** us more about Mars in the past and now.

3 Then the probe Mars 2020 **is taking off** / **will take off** from Earth in 2020.

4 It **is landing** / **will land** on Mars and study the rocks and the ground.

5 Later, another spaceship **is carrying** / **will carry** the rocks back to Earth.

6 The ESA **is also sending** / **will also send** a probe to Jupiter and its moons in 2022.

7 It **is taking** / **will take** 7.6 years for the JUpiter ICy Moons Explorer (JUICE) to travel to Jupiter.

7 **Complete these sentences in your notebook, using the words from the box.**

planets	Earth	far	kilometres	Mars
	astronauts	spaceship	take off	

Sending people to other ¹..*planets*.. is very difficult – we know that. But NASA would like to send astronauts to ²............ in 2036. Can that really happen? First, they must build the right ³............ It cannot be too heavy, or it will not ⁴............ from Earth. It must also be big and strong because it has to carry the ⁵............ and everything they will need. Mars is about 78,340,000 ⁶............ from the Earth. Astronauts have to travel for about 260 days there and 260 days back. They would not be able to get any help from ⁷............ because it is too ⁸............ away.

8 **Choose the correct answer.**

Example: 1 – b

1 What can be bad for your body?

   a gravity   **b** no gravity   **c** no light

2 How hot is it at night on Mars?

   a -100°C   **b** 0°C   **c** +100°C

3 What can we learn from space?

   a how other aliens live

   b how to live better on Earth

   c how we can live on hot and cold planets

An answer key for all questions and exercises can be found at
www.penguinreaders.co.uk

Project work

1 Imagine you are one of the first astronauts going to Mars. Write a diary and describe:
   - planning your trip
   - travelling to space
   - life on Mars.

2 Do you agree or disagree with these sentences? Prepare a debate on one of them.
   - There are UFOs, and there is alien life in space.
   - In fifty years, we will be able to live in space.
   - We have to use our money for problems on Earth, not for travelling in space.
   - We can learn some new and important things by going into space.

3 In this book you read about life in space. Find out more about space. Make a presentation about what you think tomorrow's space will be like. Work in groups and show your work to your friends.

Glossary

air (n.)
Air is everywhere, but you cannot see it. It goes into your nose and mouth.

alien (n.)
a living thing (like a person or animal) from a different *planet*

astronaut (n.)
An *astronaut* travels into space.

astronomer (n.)
An *astronomer* studies *planets* and *stars*.

atmosphere (n.)
all the gases (= things you cannot see, like *air*) in a *planet*

black hole (n.)
a place in space. If something goes into a *black hole*, it cannot come out of it again.

experiment (n.)
You do an *experiment* because you want to see what will happen, or what is true.

extrasolar planet (n.)
An *extrasolar planet* is not inside the *solar system*.

far (adj.)
not near

gas (n.)
a thing like *air*

gravity (n.)
Gravity pulls things towards other things. It is very strong.

ice (n.)
Water starts to be hard because it is very cold. Then it becomes *ice*.

kilometre (n.)
You can run a *kilometre* in about six minutes. A *kilometre* is 1000 metres.

land (v.)
to go down to the ground or water after a journey in a plane or *spaceship*

life (n.)
living things like people, animals or plants

light (adj. and n.)
1. *Light* things are not heavy. They are easy to move.
2. *Light* comes from the Sun, lamps or fire. We need it to see things.

moon (n.)
A *moon* moves in a circle. It *orbits* a *planet*. The *Moon* is in the sky at night. It is big and bright.

orbit (v.)
to move in a circle in space

planet (n.)
a large, round thing in space. Earth is a *planet*.

probe (n.)
a small *spaceship* with no one inside it. *Probes* send information to Earth.

rock (n.)
Rocks are on the ground.

satellite (n.)
We send *satellites* into space. They *orbit planets* and send pictures and information to Earth.

sign (n.)
A *sign* shows that something is there or is happening.

signal (n.)
a special sound or *light*. *Signals* give information.

solar system (n.)
a part of space with the Sun and eight *planets*. These *planets orbit* the Sun. Earth is in the *solar system*.

space station (n.)
a building in space. *Astronauts* can live there for a long time and do *experiments*.

spaceship (n.)
a plane or ship for space. A *spaceship* travels into space.

star (n.)
a very bright ball of *gas*. You see *stars* in the sky at night.

take off (v.)
A plane or *spaceship* leaves the ground and begins to fly.

telescope (n.)
A *telescope* makes things look bigger or nearer.

UFO (n.)
a strange thing in the sky. People often think that *UFOs* are *spaceships* from other *planets*.

volcano (n.)
a mountain that fire and hot *rocks* sometimes come out of

Photo credits

Cover (astronaut) © plainpicture/fstop/Caspar Benson; page 4 (astronaut) © Neil Armstrong/MPI/Getty Images; (extrasolar planet) © ESO; (moon) © Nostalgia for Infinity/shutterstock.com; (orbit) © Derplan13/shutterstock.com; (planet) © Derplan13/shutterstock.com; (probe) ©NASA/JPL-Caltech/University of Arizona; (satellite) © Andrey Armyagov/shutterstock.com; (solar system) © Derplan13/shutterstock.com; (space station) © Andrey Armyagov/shutterstock.com; (spaceship) ©NASA; (star) ©NASA Image Collection / Alamy Stock Photo; (telescope) © Vadim Sadovski/shutterstock.com; pages 6–7 (solar system) © Derplan13/shutterstock.com; page 8 (Sputnik 1) © Courtesy NSSDC, NASA; (satellite) © Andrey Armyagov/shutterstock.com; page 9 (Viking 1 probe) © ©NASA/JPL-Caltech/University of Arizona; page 10 (Cassini-Huygens spaceship) Merlin74/shutterstock.com; (Saturn and two moons) © NASA/JPL-Caltech/Space Science Institute; page 11 (Spirit and Opportunity probes) ©NASA/JPL/Cornell University, Maas Digital LLC; (Curiosity probe) © NASA/JPL-Caltech/MSSS; page 12 (Hubble telescope) © Vadim Sadovski/shutterstock.com; (supernova) © NASA images/shutterstock.com; page 13 (Chardra telescope) © bhjary/shutterstock.com; (a black hole) © Vadim Sadovski/shutterstock.com; page 14 (space) © NASA/JPL-Caltech; page 15 (Yuri Gagarin) © Heritage Images/Getty Images; (parachute) © SPUTNIK / Alamy Stock Photo; page 16 (Buzz Aldrin) © Neil Armstrong/MPI/Getty Images; (spaceship take off) ©NASA; page 17 (spaceship take off) ©NASA; page 18 (Salyut 1) © Sovfoto/ Universal images Group/Getty Images; page 19 (Skylab 1) Everett Historical/shutterstock.com; page 20 (ISS) © Andrey Armyagov/shutterstock.com; (astronauts floating) © ESA; page 21 (sleeping) © NASA; page 22 (bike and UFO) © andrey_l/shutterstock.com; page 23 (water on Earth) © Vladi333/shutterstock.com; page 24 (Venus) © NASA images/shutterstock.com; (extrasolar planet) © ESO; page 25 (radio signals) © Viktoriya/shutterstock.com; (radio telescope) © solarseven/shutterstock.com; page 26 (light signals) © Zakharchuk/shutterstock.com; (Kepler telescope) © NASA/Ames/JPL-Caltech/T Pyle; page 27 (the red planet) © mkarco/shutterstock.com; (rocks on Mars) © Guliveris/shutterstock.com; page 28 (probes travelling to Mars) © Dotted Yeti/shutterstock.com; (surface of Mars) © Alfredo Cerra/shutterstock.com; page 29 (Jupiter) © Kirschner/shutterstock.com; (moons) © mr.Timmi/shutterstock.com; page 30 (spaceship near Europa) © NASA/JPL-Caltech/Univ. of Michigan; (Ganymede) © patrimonio designs ltd/shutterstock.com; page 31 (Europa) © muratart/shutterstock.com; page 32 (Saturn) © NASA images/shutterstock.com; (Titan) © NASA/JPL-Caltech/Stéphane Le Mouélic/University of Nantes, Virginia Pasek, University of Arizona; page 33 (Enceladus) © Dotted Yeti/shutterstock.com; page 34 (extrasolar system) © Linda Brotkorb/shutterstock.com; page 35 (COROT telescope) © CNES/D. Ducros; (COROT-7b orbiting its sun) © NASA Image Collection / Alamy Stock Photo; page 36 (Kepler-186f) © NASA Ames/SETI Institute/JPL-Caltech; page 38 (buds) © ShutterProductions/shutterstock.com; page 39 (air pollution on Earth) © Artic_photo/shutterstock.com; page 40 (Australia telescope compact array) © John Masterson/CSIRO; page 41 (Earth's trees) © NASA/CC BY 2.0; page 42 (NASA in the USA) © B Christopher / Alamy Stock Photo; (space machine) © Sergey Kohl/shutterstock.com; page 43 (TESS) © NASA's Goddard Space Flight Center; page 44 (Webb telescope) © NASA; page 45 (InSight probe) © NASA/JPL-Caltech; (InSight probe) © NASA; page 46 (Mars 2020 probe) © NASA; (rocks on Mars) © NASA/JPL-Caltech/Malin Space Science Systems; page 47 (JUICE probe) © Spacecraft: ESA/ATG medialab; page 48 (NASA's Orion) © Nostalgia for Infinity/shutterstock.com; page 49 (New Glenn spaceship) © Blue Origin; (Space X's Dragon spaceship) © NASA; page 50 (Virgin Galactic spaceship) © Steve Mann/shutterstock.com; page 51 (spaceship taking off) © Alones/shutterstock.com; (spaceship interior) © Digital Storm/shutterstock.com; page 52 (spaceship with Mars in the background) © Dima Zel/shutterstock.com; (mission control) © FrameStockFootages/shutterstock.com; page 53 (astronaut back from space) © Reuters; (astronaut in space) © NASA; page 54 (astronaut from behind) © Gorodenkoff/shutterstock.com; (technician) © NASA; (Mars weather system from space) ©NASA/JPL-Caltech/MSSS; page 55 (space) © Martin Pugh